*.75

REFORMATION CROSSROADS

A Comparison of the Theology of Luther and
Melanchthon

A Comparison of the Theology of
Luther and Melanchthon

Reformation Crossroads

by Harold H. Lentz, Ph.D.

AUGSBURG PUBLISHING HOUSE
Minneapolis, Minnesota

REFORMATION CROSSROADS

A Comparison of the Theology of Luther and Melanchthon

© 1958 Augsburg Publishing House

Library of Congress Catalog Card No. 58-11863

Manufactured in the United States of America

Dedicated to my wife in appreciation of her invaluable contributions to my labors both in the congregation and in the College.

Foreword

W<small>HEN</small> God's hour had arrived for the Protestant Reformation to appear, His chief instruments within the Lutheran movement were two men who stood in marked contrast to each other. Martin Luther and Philip Melanchthon each contributed mightily to the birth of Protestantism as they cooperated in giant tasks. Yet they differed widely in their personalities, and in their thinking. With the passing centuries the name of Melanchthon is almost unknown outside Lutheranism while that of Martin Luther is familiar to the masses, regardless of denominational loyalty. However obscure the name of Melanchthon has become, his spirit continues to exist. This writer has both read and heard the statement that un-Lutheran tendencies of Melanchthon have prevailed in the Lutheran Church, causing deviations from the true genius of Lutheranism. This book is a study of this challenging subject in order to determine where, and how far, the influence of each of these two men prevails within the field of their disagreements.

Contents

At the Crossroads

Martin Luther and Philip Melanchthon, who were destined to go hand in hand as leaders of the Protestant Reformation, were first associated as colleagues on the faculty of the University of Wittenberg. When the bitter winds of Roman hatred swirled about the University the two young scholars found themselves sharing a mutual antagonism to papal policies. This common interest welded them together and developed a strong bond of friendship between them. Once when Melanchthon was desperately ill Luther went to Weimar to be near his friend, offering earnest prayers at the bedside that his life might be spared. Melanchthon later expressed the belief that he would have died if Luther had not come to him. Melanchthon even declared that he would rather die than be separated from Luther.

1

It is strange that two men of such contrasting personalities should be joined together so closely. Dia-
metrically opposed in many ways, their association
suggests the symbol of a lion lying down with a
lamb. Luther himself testified to the sharp contrast
between his personality and that of his friend by confessing: "I am rough, boisterous, stormy, and altogether warlike. I am born to fight against innumer-
able monsters and devils. I must remove stumps and
stones, cut away thistles and thorns, and clear the
wild forests, and Master Philippus comes along softly
and gently, sowing and watering with joy, according
to the gifts which God has abundantly bestowed
upon him." It is interesting to notice more particularly the differences in viewpoint between these two
men.

Luther looms as a Teutonic disciple of Augustine.
After much study and contemplation of the writings
of Paul, Luther viewed the Apostle in a new light as
a great mystic. Upon finding that Augustine shared
this view the young monk realized more than ever
the similarity between his views and those of the
great Saint after whom the Augustinian Order had
been named. He came to consider Augustine as the
greatest of the church fathers, claiming for him more
credit than all the bishops and popes "who cannot
hold a candle to him," and more than all the councils.
However, Luther did not follow him all the way,
but said that Augustine sometimes erred, and was
not to be trusted, and "although good and holy, he
was yet lacking the true faith, as well as the others"

in his life Melanchthon was accepting his master's teachings apparently *in toto,* and wrote as "a mouthpiece for Luther." The *Loci* of 1521 is a presentation of the religious concepts held in common by both men. But as the *Loci* changed its shape slowly in later editions, there became ever more evident an independent spirit which held a varying viewpoint from Luther. To see the difference in the theological views of the two men, one must look beyond the first edition of the *Loci* which was printed in 1521.

If the stars of Luther and Melanchthon had disappeared simultaneously, Luther would doubtless have predominated in history almost to the exclusion of Melanchthon as a factor of real influence upon the Lutheran church, in spite of the latter's mental dexterity and literary ability. But because of his stand in the Peasant War Luther lost some of his popular leadership to his colleague, and in the years following the Reformer's death Melanchthon had many opportunities to impress his interpretations upon earlier Lutheran views and statements. Accordingly, his importance, or the extent of his influence in moulding the future course of the church, more nearly approached that of Luther.

Thus at the head of the Protestant movement which gave birth to the Lutheran church, there were two characters of unusual ability and strength but contrasting opposites on numerous points of importance. In the succeeding years Lutheranism could follow two somewhat divergent viewpoints and still remain true to one of its founders, nor overstep the boundaries fixed by him. It is an interesting study to follow the course of Lutheran history after the death of both of its founders in an attempt to discern the influences of each man upon the church. Wherein has the church followed the Oak of Saxony, where does it bear the clear stamp of his close friend? In short, has the influence of Augustine in Luther, or the influence of the Renaissance in Melanchthon predominated in the spirit of Lutheranism during the past four centuries of its existence?

Obviously, there must be certain limits drawn in defining the field in which investigation is to be pursued. Accordingly, the scope of this book will include two important elements in Lutheran faith, the doctrine of the atonement and the principle of justification by faith, as well as two of the Lutheran symbols, the Augsburg Confession and the Formula of Concord. Reasons for selecting these particular elements are not far to seek. The doctrine of the atonement is the heart of our Christian faith, while the principle of justification by faith is the definite reaffirmation of Christian doctrine contributed by the Lutheran Reformation. The Augsburg Confession is selected because of its general acceptance by all the Lutheran bodies of the world today, something which cannot be said of other confessional works of the church. Finally, the choice of the Formula of Concord is made because it is the sole Lutheran symbol written after the death of both Luther and Melanchthon.

CHAPTER ONE

The Doctrine
of
the Atonement

FUNDAMENTALISM versus Modernism has sharply divided some denominations into two opposing camps. Again, the conflict of High Church versus Low has been a divisive issue in Protestantism. Neither of these rivalries, however, has found any soil favorable for transplanting its disputes in the Lutheran Church. In like manner, the contrasting opinions of Luther and Melanchthon, which require but little imagination in order to be seen as potential partitive factors, have never become an open issue in the Lutheran Church. Only once did the opposing views of the two founders become a cause for controversy and then the dispute was settled quickly. Some would explain this situation of prevailing peace by claiming that the views of Melanchthon never have replaced those of Luther, and that in the

7

Church's developing line of theology it has been Luther's all the way, leaving no room for any rivalry to exist. On the other hand, those who charge that the views of Melanchthon have in many instances colored Lutheran theology claim that the views of one man have superseded those of the other so quietly, without any direct intention of producing a change, that the church has been unaware of the transition. The latter explanation becomes the more reasonable when one considers the fact the the elements of Melanchthon's diverse point of view have crept into the theology of individuals and literary tradition of the Church rather than into the dogma of the Church itself.

It can scarcely be denied that all ministers in any branch of Christianity do not understand implicitly the theology of their church in its fullness. Rather it is to be admitted that only a small percentage of the membership of any ministerium is composed of real theologians. Only this small portion is aware of the many theological intricacies peculiar to its own denomination. In the Lutheran Church this is true of the real distinctions which separate Luther and Melanchthon. While theologians, in the main, have guarded the doctrines of the Church from any infiltration of Melanchthonian views, the ministers individually have not been immune to accepting interpretations from time to time at some variance with those stated in the accepted creeds and symbols of the church. The switch in viewpoint from Luther to Melanchthon has taken place, if at all, among individuals in their personal thinking, teaching, and preaching, rather than in the symbols and doctrines which the Church has accepted in its official pronouncements. Since it has been a transition on the part of individuals rather than the church itself, few have challenged the views of their fellow Lutherans on the basis that these interpretations were Melanchthonian rather than in line with Luther. At present, however, such challenges are not unknown.

There is a group of men among the Lutheran scholars of Sweden who have analyzed critically the doctrine of the Atonement as that doctrine is generally taught and believed. The University of Lund has made the largest contribution to this movement through the work of professors Gustav Aulén, Anders Nygren, and Ragnar Bring. All three have published important volumes on the subject and are outspoken in their criticism of Melanchthonian interpretations of Lutheran theology, claiming that much of the doctrinal confusion in Lutheran schools of thought is due to Melanchthon. It is the contention of this group that Luther was misunderstood, and therefore not followed, in his views relative to this cardinal doctrine of Christianity which explains the meaning of Christ's death upon the cross.

Two traditional views of the Atonement are called subjective and objective. In the objective view of the Atonement the object of Christ's atoning work is God who is reconciled through the satisfaction made to His justice. In the subjective view, the Atonement is explained as consisting essentially in a change taking place in men rather than a changed attitude on the part of God. The Swedish scholars, referred to above, point to a third view which in their opinion is commonly overlooked. This may be termed the classic idea, or *"Christus Victor,"* which teaches that God was in Christ, reconciling the world to Himself, overcoming the forces that separate God and man by victory in a divine conflict with the evil forces of the world. These men further contend that the New Testament, the Greek and Roman Fathers, Augustine and Luther in a straight line all accepted the *Christus Victor* idea. They declare that Luther revived it with his emphasis on Divine Love and his rejection of the extreme legalism which was prevalent in his day.

Gustav Aulén supports his contention that Luther accepted the classic idea of the Atonement by advancing a number of arguments which are here presented in brief epitome. He contends that (1) Luther uses images and forms of expression which are regularly characteristic of the classic idea of the Atonement. (2) One finds in Luther with regular consistency the dramatic view of the work of Christ and its meaning as a Divine conflict and victory. The term drama is employed by Aulén in its original religious and sacramental significance. In primitive times the word drama denoted simply a deed or an action. Not until later was it to signify its present meaning of an imitation of the deeds of another, actual or conceived. Furthermore, in its earliest use, drama was associated with worship as a holy deed or action, an act of adoration. The term conveys the

sense of entertainment today. Aulén uses the term
drama provisionally, in the sense that the Atonement
is a Divine conflict and victory. Returning to Aulén's
contentions concerning Luther, he declares that the
Reformer (3) always returns to the dramatic idea
in those places where it is necessary for him to express himself with the greatest possible care and
exactness, as, for instance, in the Catechisms. (4) Luther himself repeatedly assures us, with all possible
clearness, that the statements of the meaning of the
Atonement in dramatic terms give the very essence
of the Christian faith; they are *capitalia nostrae
theologiae.* (5) The dramatic view of the work of
Christ stands in organic relation with his theological
outlook as a whole. (6) As further proof it is stated
that two elements upon which Luther bases his
deepest teachings, namely "Law" and "The Wrath
of God," clearly exhibit the classic idea.

It is important to ask how Luther could be misunderstood in his concept of the Atonement. It is
inconceivable that the circle of scholars and theologians surrounding him lacked opportunity to hear
him expound his views and would not have been
brought to account for any basic disagreement. Three
reasons are advanced to explain why Luther's idea
has been misinterpreted. The doctrine of the Atonement was not a polemical issue in Luther's day and so
his statements on the subject attracted relatively little
attention. His use in a new sense of such Latin terms
as satisfaction and merit could easily be misunderstood. The classic idea has been overlooked in the be-

lief that the subjective and objective views of the Atonement were mutually exclusive. It is maintained, further, that Melanchthon was predisposed by his whole mental outlook to guide the theology of the Reformation along lines other than those Luther would have followed. By re-introducing Aristotelian philosophy, he is believed to have brought his thoughts into line with medieval scholasticism.

It appears obvious that the two men were so different in their natural characteristics that they could not fully understand each other. Luther had passed through a vastly different emotional experience in order to arrive at his theological views than had Melanchthon who was accustomed to reach his decisions purely on the basis of rationalism. Luther, once assured that he was right, could not be moved. Melanchthon was ever doubting the validity of his stand, willing often to compromise with others, stable only when under the strong hand of Luther. In the past few decades, both in Germany and in Sweden, the study of Luther has resulted in emphasizing the points of difference in these two men and the marked contrasts which they present.

Having explained how Luther could have been misunderstood, Aulén minces no words in saying that there was an immediate departure in the Lutheran Church from the views of the Reformer. He claims that Luther's contemporaries and successors reverted to the Latin doctrine, interpreting his views in the light of the traditional beliefs of the Middle Ages. As a result, Aulén declares, law came to be taken as the essential basis of man's relation to God. He quotes such men of the Reformation period as Morlin and Flacius to prove his contention. It was Morlin who wrote that "Perfect obedience of God's law, perfect fulfillment of that law, is necessary to salvation." Because of such statements, Aulén believes that the doctrine of the Atonement in Protestant Orthodoxy belongs indisputably to the Latin type, and that the classic idea of the Atonement was completely suppressed during this period of Protestant's budding life.

These charges which are leveled at the Lutheran acceptance of the doctrine of Atonement are most interesting, and worthy of consideration because of the challenge that is implied. If the contentions are true, Luther would not be a Lutheran so far as his views of this doctrine are concerned. That is to say, his views would not coincide with those of the church today. However, it should not be thought that such charges as those of Aulén are new or original with him. On the contrary, the particular line of thought which he follows resembles the reasoning of a number of men in Germany in the first half of the nineteenth century who made a determined effort to combine Lutheranism and Calvanism in a Melanchthonian church. As a reason for their attempt to unite the two groups they voiced the argument that the initial evangelical church of Germany was Melanchthonian. It was claimed that after Luther's death the so called Lutheran church was established by a group of religious zealots who were more Lutheran than Luther, and who completed their work in the Formula of Concord. Further, they proclaimed that the Palatinate, Brandenburg, Hesse and Anhalt were Calvinized only as the result of a reaction against extreme or false Lutheranism. Among those who maintained such views were Daniel Schenkal (1813-1885), leader of the Protestantenverein; Heinrich Keppe (1820-1879), Reformed theologian; and August Ebrard (1818-1887), who became well known both as an author and as a very brilliant theologian.

Returning to a critique of the theory advanced by Aulén, it is evident that he emphasizes the importance of the Law in later Lutheran theology. Indeed, one feels that he becomes extreme on this point and has over-emphasized or grossly exaggerated the Law's importance in the mind of Lutherans. If Aulén is to be believed, the Lutheran church has come to accept the Law as "the basis of man's relation to God," providing the scheme by which everything is to be interpreted, including salvation; with perfect obedience to, and fulfillment of, the Law necessary to salvation.

Such a claim certainly is flaunted in the face of considerable proof to the contrary. It is common knowledge among Lutherans that the young Luther was driven into the seclusion of the monastery by the fear of God's wrath visited upon sinful mankind, and that he emerged from the cloister willing to break with the teachings of the Roman church because he had come to see God's love which is revealed in the Incarnation and which grants forgiveness of sins and life eternal to all believers. Whereas the Law had been to the fore, he now brought the Gospel into the position of prominence, making Law subservient to it. A passage of scripture, "The just shall live by faith," breaking through his thoughts while climbing the *Scalae Sanctae* at Rome in obedience to Roman legalism, was one of the familiar incidents of his life in the chain of events which caused him to seek the reform of Roman theology. These facts have been well preserved among his followers until their knowledge is commonplace. If there has been any concerted effort by any group to steer the church from this path which emphasizes love over and above the Law, then the efforts of such a group have surely met with small success. As for the theologians, they offer proof at every turn that denies the overemphasis which Aulén claims has been given to the Law.

Textbooks used in Lutheran seminaries in America today can be taken as an example of the teaching that is being promulgated among Lutherans of America. These point out the relationship between Law and Gospel and refute the teaching that Law has anything to do with salvation. "By the Law is the knowledge of sin: by the Gospel is the knowledge of grace. It is the Gospel and not the Law that is the power of God unto salvation."

Against such teachings no cries of Nomism can justly be raised. Nomism and antinomianism are the two extreme views concerning the relation of the Law to our Christian Gospel. Nomism is simply legalism such as prevails in the Old Testament and is typified therein by the Pharisees, who believed that obedience to detailed prescriptions and regulations makes a man good. Antinomianism entirely excludes the Law. The Lutheran view does not reject the Law in its entirety as the antinomians do, nor does it observe the Law as the nomists teach should be done. Rather it acknowledges the service rendered by the Law, at the same time subordinating it to an inferior position and divorcing it from salvation as having no power of Grace. It should be clear that this is not in agreement with that view expounded by Morlin when he said, "Perfect obedience to God's Law, perfect fulfillment of God's Law is necessary to salvation." Such has never been the accepted view of the church, nor has it had any noticeable adoption on the part of individuals in the church after its rejection in Luther's day.

In all fairness, it should not be overlooked that Aulén appeals, for proof of his contentions, to Lutherans of the two extremes, Gnesio-Lutherans and Phillipists, while he quietly overlooks the largest body of Lutherans who took a stand between these extremes. Thus, he mentions prominently both Flacius and Morlin, as well as Osiander, turning to their writings at great length and quoting them in support of his claims. It is hardly justifiable to appeal to these three men because they do not fully represent Lutheranism, but rather extreme variations of it. Their teachings were rejected by the leaders of the church and as a minority whom the church refuted they can hardly be called upon to represent Lutheran views. Aulén's citation of these men as proof of his contentions that Lutheranism turned from Luther, is not adequate proof of his claims. Rather by the fact of their rejection the very opposite of his claims may be proven, for in refuting their position, which Aulén admits is non-Lutheran, the church was remaining true to Luther and preventing adulteration of his teachings.

Returning again to a critique of Aulén's presentation of the *Christus Victor* theory of the doctrine of Atonement, it may be questioned reasonably whether he has actually established a third view of the Atonement, or whether his view is not after all really the objective view, with a few alterations, expressed anew with freshness and greater clarity. That God was in Christ reconciling the world unto Himself, conquering the forces which separate God and man, is the age-old teaching of the Christian church. This idea, together with the appeasement of God's wrath, is the essence of Aulén's point of view. But rather than speak of appeasing God's wrath, he includes divine wrath as an enemy which separates God and man, and so he refers to it as being conquered in place of being appeased. Basically he seems to offer nothing new on this score. Also, in place of emphasizing judgment he places the stress upon love, but not in the least does he remove judgment from the scene. He simply asserts vigorously that love can carry us through the judgment in safety, and God is both the reconciler and the reconciled. All this presents not so much a new view of the doctrine of Atonement, as a fresh statement of an old truth.

The value of Aulén's work would seem to be two-fold. First to be mentioned is his contribution to the task of clarifying the Lutheran viewpoint on the doctrine of the Atonement and presenting it with freshness to the present age. There have long been a number of theories concerning this doctrine. To these have been given such names as the Ransom theory, the Governmental theory, the Moral Influence theory, etc. Since all these theories contain a partial truth but yet are not considered adequate or complete enough by the church, it is easy for confusion to appear when these various theories are taught. An essential task of theologians is to retain before the less informed the correct views on this subject and to point out the errors of false views. Surely *"Christus Victor"* challenges its reader to re-think his own theology and ascertain where he stands.

The second contribution of Aulén, and the one more important from the standpoint of this paper, is the historical value of his work. He points to the errors of various men and groups in the history of the Lutheran Church subsequent to the adoption of the church's official view on this doctrine of Atonement. He reveals how, to a considerable extent in the history of the church, their false views on this doctrine have led men astray. As leaders of thought they carried others with them. Aulén's volume serves as a warning that Lutheran theologians must guard against the tendency of which he speaks, namely, of turning from Luther and his teachings relative to the Atonement. He has history with which to prove his claims that men have been led astray on this point. Whether the deviation from Luther has been as pronounced as he claims is a controversial question, and probably one which can be decided only individually. However, as a fresh presentation of the Lutheran view of the Atonement Aulén's volume is of definite value, and there is no desire on the part of this writer to deprecate the worth of his contribution to the era in which it is given.

CHAPTER TWO

The Augsburg Confession

ASIDE from the ecumenical creeds few doctrinal formulations have had general acceptance by so many adherents to Protestantism as the Augsburg Confession. In addition to its unanimous adoption by Lutherans throughout the world, it has been approved by other church bodies, including Calvinism, in the edition of the Confession which is called the *Variata*. The Augustana affords a basis of comparison between Luther and Melanchthon because it has been presented to the world in many forms, the first, the work of Melanchthon writing under the guidance and with the unqualified approval of Luther, the later editions containing numerous changes and written as the independent work of Melanchthon.

At the diet of Augsburg in 1530 the Lutherans presented the first edition of the Augsburg Confession, written in Latin and German, to the Emperor, who forbade any further publication of the document.

During the sessions of the Diet reprints of the Confession appeared from unknown sources in defiance of the Emperor's command. However, these copies were filled with errors both of a typographical nature and otherwise, the copies apparently having been printed in haste and by someone not fully qualified for such work. As a result Melanchthon was led to publish, also against the command of the Emperor, an authentic copy of his work. This second official draft, containing revisions and amendments, was printed in Latin and has been called the *Editio Princeps*. Of necessity there would be some minor changes between this and the original edition because the Emperor had retained both copies given to him, and Melanchthon no longer had access to them. However, there still remained in his hands the material from which the final copies had been made ready for delivery and public reading at the Diet. Returning to these, Melanchthon could produce another copy much like the first, differing only in wording here and there. This second edition, the *Editio Princeps,* is the one accepted by the Lutheran church today.

Coincidental with the publishing of the *Editio Princeps* in Latin, Melanchthon produced a German edition which varied considerably from the Latin Text. Thus, articles twenty, twenty-two, and twenty-eight were practically new, while articles four, thirteen and eighteen were changed considerably in their wording, so that it has been called a "private work of Melanchthon" rather than the confession of the church. During the next few years Melanchthon continued to reprint the Confession, each new edition containing certain changes and variations from the preceding. Here the author overlooked the fact that once the Church had officially adopted the Confession which he had been asked to prepare, thereafter changes could rightfully be made only with the consent of the Church, and it no longer remained a personal affair with him. In 1540 he published the *Variata* edition in Latin which was to arouse so much dispute in later years. This was the first edition in which the author, in addition to altered phrases of expression, had made doctrinal statements open to challenge as differing from the doctrine presented in the original. Arguments concerning the differences between the *Variata* and the *Invariata* refer to the Latin *Editio Princeps* of 1530 as the *Invariata* and the Latin edition of 1540 as the *Variata*. The changes made in the ten year period may be grouped under three headings: (a) changes in the order of the articles, (b) enlargement and revision of some articles, mainly for the purpose of greater clarity and distinctness and simply enlarging upon earlier views without changing doctrine or thought, (c) changes which are claimed to be doctrinal differences from the original Confession. Under this heading come the subjects of Good Works, Free Will, and the Real Presence.

On the question of the real presence of Christ in the bread and wine of the Communion Table, one finds an interesting comparison between the phrases used in the two editions, 1530 and 1540. Thus, the

Invariata reads *"De coena Domini docent, quod*
CORPUS ET SANGUIS CHRISTI VERE ADSINT ET DISTRIBUAN-
TUR *vescentibus in coena Domini, et improbant secus
docentes."* The *Variata,* in much milder form, states
the thoughts thus: *"De coena Domini docent, quod*
CUM PANE ET VINO EXHIBEANTUR CORPUS ET SANGUIS
CHRISTI *vescentibus in coena Domini.* The first statement refers to the body and blood of Christ being
truly present and distributed in the communion elements, while the second statement speaks of the body
and blood being revealed (only) in the bread and
wine.

During this ten year period in his life Melanchthon
seems to have changed considerably his views concerning the real presence. In 1530, in the face of
strong objections by the Zwinglians whose doctrines
he called intolerable, he had insisted upon the phrase
"vere adsint" being included. At that time the sug-
gestion that he omit the words *"improbant secus
docentes"* was ignored. However, at the conference
in Cassel in 1535, called by Butzer of Strassburg in
the hope of uniting the Reformed with the Lutherans,
Melanchthon already shies away from Luther's conception of oral manducation. Learning that some of
the Church Fathers had taught a symbolical conception of the Lord's Supper he began to appreciate the
Reformed viewpoint. While not rejecting the Lutheran doctrine he did lose an appreciation of the
difference between Lutheran and Reformed views
on this subject.

In 1540 Zwinglianism was no longer a distinct

threat to the Lutheran Church in Germany. This fact, together with Melanchthon's desire to unite all Protestants in Germany under a mild form of Lutheranism led him to speak with greater restraint.

His continuous changing of the *Loci* affords another basis for weighing the changing views of Melanchthon. In 1535 he had published a new edition of the *Loci* in which he emphasized repentance and good works in a manner characterized by Zoeckler as that of synergism, and which the professor believes is apparent in the *Variata*. Kolde likewise raises the cry of synergism against Melanchthon, pointing out, further, that in his emphasis on repentance (article V) and good works (article XX) this strain is especially noticeable.

Not for a period of twenty years, however, was the Lutheran Church to become aware of the divergence of the *Variata* from established Lutheran doctrine. And then such recognition was to come only after opponents of the church had openly made such claims, and after the changing circumstances of the times made the statements of 1540 embarrassing for the church. When the Calvinists determinedly rejected the Real Presence and chances for union were known to have disappeared, the Lutherans regretted the concessions which the *Variata* had made during a period when attempts toward a union had developed a conciliatory attitude on the part of all. In 1540 Dr. Eck had protested against the *Variata* as a work altered in doctrine from the edition of 1530, but his statements apparently were not taken seriously by the Lutherans. In 1560 a disputation was held in Weimar between Victor Strigel and M. Flacius on the subject of the doctrine of Free Will. At this debate Flacius insisted there was a material difference between the two editions of Melanchthon's work. In 1561 the Protestant Princes of Germany, gathered at Naumburg to decide on a confessional basis for Lutheranism to present to the Council of Trent if they should be called before that body, argued over which of the two editions should be accepted. This dispute among laymen ended in a compromise stand. In the following years the body of doctrine collected by the various German states included the *Invariata* of 1530 in a great many instances. Finally, Elector August of Saxony, because of the persistent appeals of the Melanchthonians and Crypto-Calvinists to the *Variata,* was led to cooperate in the task of creating the Formula of Concord. The appearance, in 1580, of the Book of Concord, in which were assembled all the Lutheran symbols in a single volume, found universal acceptance in adopting the first edition of the Confession instead of the *Variata.* Since that date the importance of (and the knowledge of) the *Variata* has steadily diminished.

Another point of comparison between the two reformers revolves about their concept of the Church. To the writer of this book it appears that their differences on this subject have been all but overlooked in America, thus increasing the possibility of following Melanchthon's views on the subject without realizing it. Luther had a spiritual conception of the

Church which led him to view it as a unity wherever found—among Anglicans, Lutherans, Reformed,
Catholics or any other group. The Church, to him,
was the body of Christ. This spiritual body is draped
by the various organizations as clothes drape a body
but yet do not become part of the body. While the
church may take many forms in various denominations, these forms are not the Church itself which is
spiritual. The true Church, according to Luther, is
the communion of saints, a kingdom invisible over
which Christ rules as the invisible head through the
invisible power of His Word. This Church exists
wherever God's Word has found a place to abide, but
its existence is appreciated only by faith. It remains
hidden for the senses.

Karl Rieker explains that "What we call visible
church, this complex of external institutions, congregations, dioceses, synods, ministerial offices, church
governments—this *societas externarum rerum ac
rituum*, as the Apology says, is from Luther's point of
view nothing else than 'a piece of world' and it stands
in no closer relation to the invisible church than does
any *Gemeinschaft*, gathered in Christ's name."

Melanchthon thought of the church not so much
as a unity as much as in the sense of a dualism—a
church visible and a church invisible. Thus Dr. J. O.
Evjen writes: "Luther's fundamental view of the
Church was presented both in the Augsburg Confession and in the Apology; but Melanchthon prepared,
in both, a way for the differentiation according to
which there is a church in the 'real' and in the

broader meaning *(ecclesia proprie dicta* and *ecclesia large dicta).* This distinction remained foreign to Luther."

Naturally this true Lutheran concept of the Church is in contradistinction to the teachings of the Roman Catholic church with its emphasis upon externals. To Romanists, Luther's concept would appear to be a fantastic dream, a non-reality. But the Apology to the Augsburg Confession proclaims: "We are speaking not of an imaginary church, which is found nowhere; but we say and know certainly that this church, wherein saints live, is and abides truly on earth." Professor Herman Sasse of Erlangen in his notable volume, *Here We Stand,* comments on this statement in *The Apology* thus: "To believe this church means to believe that in, with, and under the manifestations of the historical church, the *Una Sancta,* the Body of Christ, is hidden, and yet is present, in the world as a reality.

"This explains why old Lutheranism was so extraordinarily concerned about the church which was in existence. Even in the deteriorating church of the late Middle Ages, even in the church of the Renaissance popes, it recognized the church of Christ. For even in this church the Gospel and Sacraments of Jesus Christ, the marks of the existence of the true church, were still nominally present. The church of that particular time was not judged any differently from the church of the whole Middle Ages. In those last centuries the Antichrist may well have occupied the papal chair, but his throne was placed in the sanctuary, in the temple of God. Even when the medieval church fell upon its most evil days, it still preserved the Gospel, Holy Baptism, and the Sacrament of the Altar, albeit the latter was deprived of one kind and mutilated by 'this dragon's tail, the Mass,' which has 'produced manifold abominations and idolatries' (quoted from Luther in the Smalcald Articles). Anyone who maintains that Luther and the Lutheran Church erred in believing that the church of Christ existed even in the papal church of this time, must, to be consistent, deny that the church of Christ was to be found in the Roman Church of the Middle Ages. . . . In fact, the logical conclusion would be that the papal church, as the 'synagogue of Satan,' can have absolutely nothing to do with the church of Christ.

"The Lutheran Church deliberately rejected this view. And it did so, not because of any inherent inclination toward compromise or halfway measures, but because of its conception of the church—a conception which enabled the Lutheran Church, even obliged it, to acknowledge that the true church of Christ could also be found in the Roman Church."

Having presented briefly some of the subjects upon which Melanchthon disagreed with Luther, it is well to return to the thesis of this book which is concerned with the influence of each man upon the church in the many years following his death. Note has already been made on a previous page that in compiling the Book of Concord of 1580 it was the *Invariata* of 1530 and not the *Variata* of 1540 which was included. This is, of course, indication of the superiority of Luther's influence upon the church at that time. This is by no means final nor conclusive proof, however. How did the two editions fare in other lands?

In Austria the peace of Augsburg of 1555, based on the principle of *cuius regio, eius religio,* had denied freedom to the Evangelicals under Ferdinand I. In 1564, when Maximilian II was Emperor, some of the estates of lower Austria presented the request to him that they be permitted to retain the Christian religion which they held according to the Augsburg Confession which had been delivered to the Emperor Charles V. This was an appeal on the basis of the *Invariata.* Further, when the Emperor gave permission to the lords and knights in 1568 to hold private services according to the Augsburg Confession he stated expressly that the concession applied only to those who accepted the *Invariata.* The same action was taken in upper Austria. There Maximilian II assured his subjects that in religious matters he expected his subjects carefully to avoid all sects contrary to the Augsburg Confession of 1530. Repeatedly in years following this same spirit was expressed, with the Augsburg Confession of 1530 being named as the norm and with admonitions not to encourage sects or to stray from the Confessional teachings. Inner Austria consistently followed a similar pattern.

In Moravia the Augsburg Confession became an accepted doctrine on the part of many individual congregations. While in the main the official references by these communities were simply to the Confession in general, it is found that the congregation in Sternberg expressly stated that preaching and teaching was to be "According to the sole norm and guide of the holy divine Scriptures . . . and the unaltered Augsburg Confession."

So far it appears that other nations were following the lead of Germany in rejecting the Melanchthonian digressions of the later editions of the Confession. Hungary, however, was the land which proved an exception for there one can note a swing toward Melanchthon. Leonhard Stoeckal, an admirer of Melanchthon, had reorganized a Latin school at Bartfield in 1539 which became the center of Evangelical life. The Hungarian diet in 1548 adopted a strong law against Baptists and Sacramentarians which led five cities to prepare a confession of their faith lest they be confused with the Sacramentarians. The five free cities were Eperies, Bartfield, Klein-Zeben, Kaschau and Leutschau, and Leonhard Stoeckal was chosen to prepare the Confession. Since these same cities had, in 1546, voted that instructions in schools and churches was to be in harmony with the Augsburg Confession, it is not surprising to find this confession, called the *Pentapolitana,* to be pretty much a reproduction of the first part of the Augsburg Confession. When one studies carefully, against the background of the situation then existing, the changes made in the *Pentapolitana* it does not seem possible to say that there is material digression from the Augsburg Confession. It is of extreme importance to the subject of this chapter that Lutheran pastors of Hungary were pledged to the entire Book of Concord, containing the *Invariata* edition of the Augsburg Confession.

In succeeding years religious wars and persecutions brought many changes, while the two World Wars made major alterations in the map of Europe. Under the suppression of Communism the churches in many countries exist precariously and the constant threat of state interference in all their internal affairs places these churches in a fluid state. It can only be said that prior to this period of uncertainty certain conditions existed in regard to the acceptance of the Augsburg Confession. This is true of Poland as well as Hungary.

In Poland there was a definite impact of what might be known as a Melanchthonian influence, principally in the area designated as Little Poland as distinguished from Great Poland. The former gives evidence of defection from Luther in numerous ways. One instance is the synod of Pinczow, when, in 1550 a writing compiled by Bucer, Melanchthon and Hedio, and termed the Cologne Reformation was adopted. Later this area came under the influence of Swiss theologians. Great Poland maintained close relations with Lutheranism through the Lutheran Duke Albrecht of Prussia, but there were many other influences which tended to adulterate the faith. There was verbal allegiance to the Augsburg Confession without copies of the Confession being available in the Polish language. When so-called translations did appear they bore numerous changes from the *Invariata.* Not until 1595 when Lutheranism had been in Poland for fifty years, did the first edition of the Latin *Editio Princeps* appear in a Polish translation.

The Scandinavian countries should be considered because of the strength of Lutheranism in those lands. In Denmark, the *Kirchenordinantie* of 1537, written by Bugenhagen and Hans Tausen, became the official doctrinal statement of the church when it was adopted at the Reichstag of Odense in 1539. Though in harmony with the Augsburg Confession, the *Kirchenordinantie* did not so much as mention it. The first translation of Augustana appeared in 1533, the work of Joergen Sadolin, first Evangelical bishop, and it is believed the *Editio Princeps* was the basis of his work, as it was also for the next edition which appeared much later, in 1618. This one, by Oluff Jacobsoen, was given the approval of the Danish church.

Norway simply followed Denmark as part of the same empire. Sweden, where the early Reformation found it difficult to gain a strong foothold, did not adopt the Augsburg Confession until the Council of Upsala in 1593. However, at that time it stipulated that it was the unaltered Augsburg Confession which was adopted as the confessional basis. Finland, as a part of Sweden, had the same confessional basis as the mother land.

Just when an English translation of the Augsburg Confession first appeared is a question which is not settled definitely. There is a copy in the British

Museum, the work of Richard Tavener, which was printed in 1536. If not the earliest English translation, this is among the very first. This translation was based on the second Latin Edition of 1531 and is considered an official edition of the Kingdom because it was brought about by none less than Thomas Cromwell, the Lord Privy Seal, Viceregent to the King's Highness, Secretary of State and Minister of Spiritual Affairs, and was printed with royal permission. A scholar of the highest rank, Tavener presented to English speaking people an edition which is still recognized. Near the close of the Nineteenth century the three Synods which later were to form the United Lutheran Church in America, in printing a translation of the Augsburg Confession, used Tavener as the basis of their work. As we have noted previously, this work of Tavener was founded on the 1531 edition, not the later Melanchthonian editions of the Confession.

In the Netherlands the Reformation met with ever changing conditions. For a time the Evangelicals would be permitted freedom of worship and then for a period the privilege would be denied. Through many years this ever changing state of affairs continued. Many theological works disappeared each time the Evangelicals were banished and it is difficult to trace the fate of the Augsburg Confession during those stormy years. That there were some editions of the Confession based on the later Melanchthonian works seems probable but has not been proven to date. After the Duke of Parma, in 1585, captured

Antwerp and gave the Evangelicals the bitter choice of becoming Catholic or leaving, Amsterdam became the center of Dutch Lutheranism and has remained in the position of leadership since that time, having nearly half the Lutheran population of Holland today. There in 1597, was published a Church Order which runs in direct line of descent to the present Lutherans of Amsterdam. This Order stated: "The Pastors of the congregations shall regulate and determine all their teachings and preachings by the rule of the divine Word, the biblical, prophetical and apostolical writings, and according to our Symbolical Books, to wit the unaltered Augsburg Confession . . . the Apology of the same, the Smalcald Articles, the Formula of Concord, together with both Catechisms of Luther, and shall not teach or preach anything contrary to the same, be it privately or publicly, nor shall they introduce or use new phrases which are at variance with the same, or contradict them." Revisions appeared later, almost every decade, but this paragraph was not changed.

There is little to guide one in an investigation of the treatment accorded the Augsburg Confession in France. Several early editions have been discovered but their origin of publication is undetermined. Some follow the *Variata*, others the *Invariata*. This fact simply shows that to some extent the influence of Melanchthon is to be noted among French Lutherans of an early day. However, Lutherans in France have never been a strong body and are not given further attention at this time.

Earliest Lutherans in America were those few who were numbered among the Dutch colonists of New Netherland, later, under British rule, renamed New York. Next came the Swedish Lutherans who settled in Delaware. Reorus Torkillus who was a member of the second Swedish expedition which arrived in 1640 bears the distinction of being the first Lutheran pastor to work among the settlers in America. In 1642 the Rev. John Campanius arrived, devoting himself to the Indians for whom he translated the Catechism of Luther into their own tongue. German immigrants to the New World settled in Pennsylvania. In 1694 two men who were to make large contributions to the life of the German Lutherans in America arrived at the newly founded Germantown in Pennsylvania. The men were Henry Koester and Daniel Falchner. "The first German Lutheran service in Germantown, in fact, in America, was conducted by Koester in 1694."

When Lutherans had been in America for a whole century there was still no organization of the separate congregations, scattered far and wide over the vast territory that stretched along the Atlantic seaboard, into a Synod or Ministerium. The need for a larger organization, incorporating the many separate congregations, was being realized increasingly. Count Von Zinzendorf, an exile from Saxony, arrived in America in 1741 to take up his home among the Lutherans in Pennsylvania. He dreamed of a union of the congregations belonging to several denominations, including Baptists, Mennonites, Reformed and Lutherans. His efforts finally resulted in the *Unitas Fratrum* or Moravian Brotherhood, a group composed of some from each of the four denominations mentioned previously, who withdrew to form their separate organization. Though this might be considered a loss to the Lutherans of America, they were to gain more than they relinquished, for the result of Zinzendorf's activity was to awaken authorities at Halle to the necessity of church organization in America. To meet the need, Henry Melchior Muhlenberg was dispatched, arriving in Philadelphia on November 25, 1742. His prodigious labors and splendid ability bore much fruit; especially did he excell as an organizer during a period when organization was considered the basic need. Due to his efforts the first Lutheran Ministerium came into being in Pennsylvania, and to him has been applied the title Patriarch of the Lutheran Church in America.

During these years when Lutheranism was being transplanted from the several nations of the Old World into the new colonies, how did the Augsburg Confession fare? Was it the Altered or Unaltered edition which was brought across the Atlantic and adopted for use by the churches in America? With no definite organizations developed in the new land, no doctrinal statements were adopted and as a result it is difficult to ascertain the treatment given the Augustana. Some hints of the Confession's acceptance are given, however. For instance, in the Dutch Colony of New York the Lutherans protested against the forced allegiance to the Reformed church which

Governor Stuyvesant demanded. Lutherans had been forbidden to hold meetings in private homes and were forced to have their children baptized by Reformed pastors. In protesting to the Governor, they called themselves "adherents of the Unaltered Augsburg Confession." Doubtless the Swedish and German congregations followed their mother churches in the adoption and application of the Confession. The dearth of specific references to the edition of the Confession used by the early churches shows it was not a great problem to the early settlers. Later, however, the calm was to disappear and a great storm gather over the followers of Luther in North America, and the focal point of the controversy was to be the Augsburg Confession.

America witnessed the most concerted effort among Lutherans to make a deliberate break from the teachings of Luther, including an attempt to adopt a modern recension of the Augsburg Confession. In the middle of the Nineteenth century, under able leadership, a movement to develop an "American Lutheranism" was inaugurated. Such action is not surprising when one considers the background of the Lutheran Church in America. Indeed, it is claimed that if those men who led the movement had not taken the action they did, someone else would have done so, either then or later, for the times and conditions were most favorable for developing just such a movement and there was a problem arising within the church which had to be faced sooner or later.

Lutherans came to America from Holland, Norway, Sweden, Germany and other countries. Thus they were not in complete accord on many rites and practices, nor did they all agree on the adoption of the same Lutheran symbols, some holding to the Augsburg Confession alone, others confessing all the symbols in the Book of Concord. Because of the independence of the various German states even the German Lutherans in America did not find themselves in complete accord. Consequently, one finds in America in earlier days, a great many Lutheran groups, descendants of a number of European races, with varying degrees of loyalty to Lutheran Confessions. Added to this was the fact that they were cut off from the home base, with only a few Lutheran schools and seminaries on American soil, surrounded here by a great many denominations who differed widely both in doctrine and practice from their own religious heritage. Finally, a second generation of Lutherans were now in the leadership of the church. They were men who had been raised on American soil and spoke the English language. They felt the lack of Lutheran literature in English and to meet the deficiency were forced to turn to authorities, commentaries, and aids in the study of theology which the churches around them afforded. They received their meagre store of knowledge of Lutheran theology second hand, through writers loyal to other denominations. The lack of Lutheran schools on this side of the Atlantic made the situation critical. "The seminary course was very brief, and the teaching scarcely rose above, if it equaled, the standard of the better catechetical instruction." College, and often seminary, training of Lutheran pastors was received at denominational schools which were not Lutheran. In the midst of such a situation it is not surprising to find the call arising among some of these men for an American Lutheranism, one breaking at many points from the spirit of the old Lutheran Church.

Leader of this modern movement was S. S. Schmucker who had graduated from Princeton Theological Seminary. He is regarded as a man of great talent and splendid ability who gave the movement the type of leadership necessary to insure its success if ever it was to prevail. Associated with him were Dr. Benjamin Kurtz and Dr. Samuel Sprecher, later president of Wittenberg College. Their effort culminated in a Definite Synodical Platform which was an attempt to unite all Lutherans in America on the basis of the platform set forth. The document made some concessions to surrounding denominations as an accommodation on the part of the Lutheran Church to the American spirit. It appeared anonymously in 1855 but almost at once the work of Schmucker was recognized. Included in the Platform was an American Recension of the Augsburg Confession. It made changes in its interpretation of Lutheran theology on such important items as the sacraments of the Lord's Supper and of baptism.

That this Platform represents a Melanchthonian tendency in America is obvious and such charge was immediately raised against it. It is characteristic of

Melanchthon's irenic and conciliatory attitude, and his willingness to sacrifice differences of opinion for the sake of unity. The article on the Lord's Supper is most typical of Melanchthon's views on this point where the two reformers were openly in disagreement, as this paper has previously noted. Professor Sprecher himself, one of the three leaders of the movement producing the Definite Platform of 1855 and possibly a contributor to the work of drawing up the articles, later admitted their Melanchthonian nature. Before his death he repudiated the spirit of the Platform by writing in the Lutheran Evangelist: "It is true that I did once think the Definite Synodical Platform — that modification of Lutheranism which perhaps has been properly called the culmination of Melanchthonianism—desirable and practical, and that I now regard all such modification of our creed as hopeless. In the meantime an increased knowledge of the spirit, methods, and literature of the Missouri Synod has convinced me that such alterations are undesirable; that the elements of true Pietism—that a sense of the necessity of personal religion and the importance of personal assurance of salvation—can be maintained in connection with a Lutheranism unmodified by the Puritan element."

At one time it appeared that American Lutheranism was to develop into a majority movement among Lutherans, but such an idea quickly vanished upon the appearance of the Platform, for it received little response of a sympathetic nature. Three small synods adopted it, five synods condemned it, and the other fifteen synods either rejected or totally ignored the document. It was condemned everywhere in the strongest language. The "Crisis in American Lutheran Theology" witnessed Luther and Melanchthon locked in a death struggle and from the conflict Luther appears to have emerged victorious. From the standpoint of the church itself there was to be no adulteration of accepted, orthodox doctrine. This was one of the clearest conflicts in which the two reformers were ever opposed; and it strongly rejected Melanchthon. Today the three great bodies of Lutherans in America all subscribe to the Unaltered Augsburg Confession.

Admitting all this, however, one should not be led to think that no trace of Melanchthonianism would remain. Earlier it was mentioned that the church can officially adopt a certain stand but this is no guarantee that the same position either will be understood by, or find strict adherence on the part of, all individuals in the church or its ministerium. In this case the protagonists of an American Lutheranism were not immediately eradicated nor their influence completely stamped out. Their stand is one which some men from time to time are almost bound to assume as a natural human course. One has only to listen in order to hear "American Lutheranism" in its modern form suggested today. It now assumes the form of a denial of the adequacy of historic creeds and symbols to meet modern situations and current problems.

There are signs that the spirit of Melanchthon

lives on among Lutherans of America today. Occasionally someone rises to point to such indications
but in general there is little said or written on the
subject. Mention has been made earlier of the contrasting conception of the church held by the two
men. If Luther's view of the church prevailed today,
a view which recognized the body of Christ even
in the Catholic church, it would seem there would
be less of a critical attitude and of a spirit of lofty
aloofness in some of Lutherans in America toward
other groups of Lutherans at the present time. Refusal
of one body to have fellowship—in prayer, in the pul-
pit, or at the altar—with any other denomination or
even with another branch of their own denomination,
is a stand which will be increasingly more difficult to
vindicate on Lutheran grounds.

Looking back over this chapter it is interesting,
in summary, to take a synoptic view of the course of
the Augsburg Confession and the treatment accorded
it in various lands. The Lutheran church in Germany
was for a half a century unaware of the differences
of Melanchthon and Luther, revealed in the two editions of the Confession. By the time the church realized the variations, both views had spread to other
lands where they were running their course side by
side. It was the acceptance of the altered edition
by opponents of Lutheranism which led the church
in Germany to reject it. What the ultimate outcome
of the two editions would have been had there been
no outside interference, is a subject of interest but
one confined to the realm of pure conjecture. Austria

and Moravia followed Luther quite definitely, while Hungary and Poland were under Melanchthon's influence. Denmark failed to take much notice of the Augustana, nor did Norway, which followed the mother country. The same is true of Sweden and Finland.

England went back to the original in producing the translation by Tavener. In the Netherlands, also, the unaltered edition dominated, while in France the evidence of Melanchthonian influence has been noted. Finally, America has remained officially with the early edition, but the tremendous influence of Melanchthon is shown in the fact that during the Nineteenth century a crisis could arise which was the result of a conflict of the views of the two Reformers.

CHAPTER THREE

The Doctrine
of Justification
by Faith

O<small>NE</small> characteristic of Luther which cannot be overlooked if the Reformer is to be rightly understood, is his conception of the depravity of man in the sight of God, together with man's utter inability to secure forgiveness and salvation for himself. With the emotions of a man over whom there hangs the sentence of death, Luther inquired into the meaning of *justitia Dei*. Because this problem lay heavily on his soul, driving him to find the way and meaning of salvation, he entered the monastery, and continuing his search there with still greater zeal, he arrived at last at his view of Justification by Faith. It was his supreme contribution to Christian doctrine and life and the cornerstone of his reformation movement. With the greatest joy and peace he emerged from his struggle to find the way to salvation. Feel-

44

ing the weight of his sins lifted from his soul as he
sensed the meaning of his discovery, he had an
experience somewhat mystical and ineffable. He
believed a revelation had been given to him by the
Holy Ghost and he writes about the bliss of that
moment when "I felt as if I were altogether born
anew and as if I had entered paradise through open
portals." Also, the experience gave him a revealing
insight into the meaning of the righteousness of
God which led him to hate and fear the righteousness no longer, but instead to love and cherish it.
Continuing to describe the moment of his discovery,
he writes: "The entire Bible suddenly looked different to me. I ran through it, so far as I could remember it, and gathered a large number of similar
expressions, like 'work of God,' that is, what God
works in us; 'power of God,' that is, the power with
which He makes us powerful; 'wisdom of God,' that
is, the wisdom with which He makes us wise . . .
The more I hated the phrase, 'righteousness of God,'
before, so much the more precious and sweet it
was to me now. Thus that passage in Paul became in
truth the portal to paradise."

Luther believed that he had uncovered a Gospel
truth long obscured and hidden from the people.
It appeared to him to be the very heart of the
Gospel which had been lost and that his theory of
Justification by Faith was the rock foundation of
Christian doctrine. Therefore, the Apology to the
Augsburg Confession speaks of Justification as "the
chief topic of Christian doctrine . . . which is of

especial service for the clear, correct understanding of the entire Holy Scriptures, and alone shows the way to the unspeakable treasure and right knowledge of Christ, and alone opens the door to the entire Bible." Further, the Smalcald Articles say of Justification that "nothing can be yielded or surrendered, even if heaven and earth and all things sink to ruin." Again the Formula of Concord quotes Luther with the statement: "If only this article is kept pure, the Christian church also remains pure and is harmonious and without all sects; but if it does not remain pure, it is not possible to resist any error or fanatical spirit."

In seeing God's righteousness conferred upon man in the form of Godly power and Godly wisdom, Luther comprehended a royal righteousness of man. He understood that now in all truth our faith in Christ makes us "sons of God," or "heirs of God and joint heirs with Christ." His insight was carried over to the German people, giving them a sense of royal freedom which is a mark of those times, but which seems to be less prominent in later times. Professor Herman Sasse speaks of the "jubilation which used to fill many thousands of hearts when everybody sang Luther's hymn, 'Rejoice, ye ransomed of the Lord!' and when, by means of this and many another similar hymn, the doctrine of the sinner's justification (this alleged phantom of ideas fashioned by theological theorists) rooted itself in the souls of the simple people. These people were learning for the first time what the Gospel is. The old words of the liturgy, the Scripture quotations, the prayers, and the hymns of the church took on new life for them. Now for the first time they understood what it is to believe in Jesus Christ. They grasped the meaning of the forgiveness of sins and they learned the truth of the words in the Catechism: 'For where there is remission of sins, there are also life and salvation.' They knew what the Word of God is, and that one could literally live by the Word of God; in fact, that one could not live without it. Never in the course of German history has any teaching been proclaimed which has so stirred the people, so deeply moved them, as the teaching which Luther brought them in the years of the Reformation."

Whereas the mediaeval church viewed Justification as something dispensed by the church and through the channels of its vast organization, Luther taught a priesthood of all believers, wherein the church is not a mediating factor but rather each man, through faith, lays hold on the justification of Christ for himself.

The Roman church taught a justification which was achieved by penance, confession, and the performance of meritorious good works imposed by the priest, including prayer, almsgiving, and maceration. Luther believed that a person could go through such a process without ever having a real sense of pardon. Luther's view of the Justification as a sense of pardon and a desire to do good works has been stated simply but graphically in these words: "The faith, however, which is the gift of God makes the believer see in the Christ who is there before him a revelation of God's Fatherly love which gives him the sense of pardon, and at the same time excites in him the desire to do all manner of loving service. He is like the forgiven child who is met with tenderness when punishment was expected, and in glad wonder resolves never to be naughty again —so natural and simple is the Reformation thought." T. M. Lindsay admirably sums up the striking contrasts between Medieval and Reformation conceptions of Justification in the following manner:

(1) The Reformation thought always looks at the comparative imperfection of the works of believers, while admitting that they are good works; the medieval theologian, even when bidding men disregard the intrinsic value of their good works, always looks at the relative *perfection* of these works.

"(2) The Reformer had a much more concrete idea of God's grace—it was something special, particular, unique—because he invariably regarded the really good works which men can do from their relative imperfection; the medieval theologian looked at the relative perfection of good works, and so could represent them as something congruous to the grace of God which was not sharply distinguished from them.

"(3) These views led Luther and the Reformers to represent faith as not merely the receptive organ for the reception and appropriation of justification through Christ, but, and in addition, as the active instrument in all Christian life and work—faith is our life; while the mediaeval theologians never attained this view of faith.

"(4) The Reformer believes that the act of faith in his justification through Christ is the basis of the believer's assurance of his pardon and salvation in spite of the painful and abiding sense of sin; while the medieval theologian held that the divine sentence of acquittal which restored a sinner to a state of grace resulted from the joint action of the priest and the penitent in the Sacrament of Penance, and had to be repeated intermittently."

Although the relationship of Justification and Predestination is not always clear, the two doctrines are closely connected. It is at this point—the relationship of Justification and Predestination—that the Reformed and the Lutheran branches of Protestantism separate. The place held by Justification in the Lutheran church would appear to be held by Predestination in the Reformed churches. Compare the similarity of phrases in two confessions, one from each body. The Apology of the Augsburg Confession ascribes to Justification the gift of a "necessary and most abundant consolation to devout consciences," while the Westminster Confession speaks of the "abundant consolation" afforded by the "high mystery of predestination." Both doctrines assert that we are saved by Grace alone, and are subscribed to by both Lutherans and Reformed. But as Professor Sasse points out: "it makes a great deal of difference which of the two doctrines is placed in the foreground. It makes a difference whether Predestination is seen in the light of Justification, or Justification in the light of Predestination.

"The Reformed Church does the latter. Its thinking about God proceeds from the fact that God dwells in brightness which no one can approach, in majestic elevation above everything finite, temporal, and human, separated from the world by a deep chasm which divides the finite from the infinite, the creatures from his Creator and Lord. His inscrutable, sovereign will is the cause of everything that happens, the cause also of man's good and evil fortune. Everything must contribute to His glory; creation and salvation, judgment and perfection, eternal life and eternal death. Before the foundations of the world were laid, He decided upon the unfathomable decrees which predetermined the fate of all creatures. Even the fall of Adam was not merely foreseen, but predetermined. With sovereign arbitrariness, and yet with inconceivable justice—for God's will is always just—He selected a part of mankind for salvation and doomed the rest to damnation. For the sake of those elected to salvation, and for them alone, the eternal Son of God became man. The call to repentance and the promise of grace really applies only to these. They alone are received as children of God in Baptism. What determines our salvation, therefore, is the decree which God made before all time. The justification of the sinner for Christ's sake is only a confirmation of the salvation which has long since been effected.

"Utterly different is the way in which Lutheran

theology speaks of God. Lutheran theology is also
aware that God dwells in brightness which no one
can approach. It also recognizes the vast, boundless distance which separated the creature from his
Creator. It knows, too, about the God of Predestination: 'This God who makes us responsible for de-
mands which we cannot fulfill, who asks us questions
which we cannot answer, who created us for good
and yet leaves us no other choice than to do evil—
this is the *Deus absconditus*. This is the God of
absolute Predestination. This is the God who hard-
ened Pharaoh's heart, who hated Esau even before he
was born, the Potter who fashions pots and before
whom one shrinks—and who, nevertheless, thunders
in pitiless sovereignty at these unhappy creatures,
"*Tua culpa!* Thine is the guilt!" In this way Professor Elert sets forth the view of the God of Predestination which Luther develops in his great work
against Erasmus, the view to which Luther clung
to the end of his days. Luther himself probably had
a far livelier sense of the utter unfathomableness
of divine majesty and the sovereign will of God, and
probably felt the pitiless rigor of God's wrath more
keenly than Calvin, who never experienced the de-
spair of 'surely sinking into hell' and who always
spoke about these theological ideas with something
of a learned humanist's philosophical repose. But
tremendous as this terrible reality of the 'hidden
God' is to Luther and to the Lutheran Church, they
know something even more tremendous, something
which grips the heart even more profoundly, some-

thing which goes even further in surpassing human thought. This is the fact that this hidden God has revealed Himself. He has stepped out of the profound darkness behind which, to our eyes, the brightness was concealed so that no one could draw near. He has come to us across the boundless distance which separates the Creator from His fallen creature, and has told us His name.

> Ask ye, who is this?
> Jesus Christ it is,
> Of Sabaoth Lord,
> And there's none other God.

". . . . When the Gospel says that 'God so loved the world that He gave His only begotten Son, that whosoever believeth on Him should not perish, but have eternal life,' the divine mercy is actually extended to the whole world, not to the elect alone. *All* who believe on Him shall be saved. The call of the Incarnate, 'Come unto me *all!*' means what it says. 'And this call of God, which is made through the preaching of the Word, we should regard as no delusion, but know that thereby God reveals His will, *viz.*, that in those whom He thus calls He will work through the Word, that they may be enlightened, converted, and saved.' When Calvin asserts that God has resolved, in His eternal decree, to communicate the Word sometimes 'to those whom He only enlightens for a season, and afterward forsakes . . . and strikes with a greater blindness,' his speculation no longer rests on the New Testament testimony about God. Thus he is obliged to inter-

pret the statement of Paul that 'God would have all
men to be saved and come to the knowledge of
the truth' in such a way as to reconcile it with
his view that God does *not* wish all men to be saved.
That this is doing violence to the Bible is quite obvious."

We have discussed at considerable length the
Lutheran idea of Justification by Faith, especially
as contrasted with the Mediaeval and with the Reformed conception. How then did Melanchthon
differ from Luther on this cardinal doctrine of Lutheran faith? This is no simple question, easily answered. Whether Melanchthon differed at all can
hardly be established with any degree of conviction. It is not possible to lay one's finger on any
statements of his in which he openly makes an exception to any of Luther's statements on Justification
by Faith, as he did in reference to Luther's view of
oral manducation. One must look for a *change of
emphasis* in Melanchthon's treatment of Justification
by Faith rather than for a definite disagreement.

Melanchthon was always inclined to stress the importance of good works, occasionally leading one
to think he held to the necessity of good works for
salvation, a charge which is sometimes leveled
against him. He had a humanistic strain inherited
from his relative and teacher, Erasmus, which in-
duces some to say that through Melanchthon Humanism entered the Reformation.

With his leaning toward ethics and the Natural
Law and stress on life and good works, Melanchthon

would naturally be expected to carry such emphasis over into the doctrine of Justification by Faith. Here we see a tendency on his part to lay stress upon sanctification. Koeberle, in his volume, *Quest for Holiness,* describes this trait of Melanchthon's. It is the crux of Melanchthon's differences with Luther on this doctrine.

In *An Introduction to Lutheran Symbolics* it is recorded that "The Melanchthonian, George Major, made the statement: 'Good works are necessary for salvation.' This seemed to agree with the words of our article (VI of the Augsburg Confession) 'that this faith is bound to bring forth good fruits and that it is necessary to do good works.' But the danger was the Melanchthonian synergism as a special interest back of that statement. So Nic. Amsdorf, the extreme follower of Luther, opposed the statement: 'Good works are injurious to salvation.' Melanchthon, replying, called this a 'cynical and cyclopic nonsense.' The Formula of Concord, in Article IV, settled the controversy by teaching that good works are necessary not in the article of justification, but in the article of sanctification; and that good works may become injurious when 'we rely upon those works to merit justification before God.' One must read these discussions in both the Solid Declaration and the Epitome to be impressed with the manner in which the Lutheran Church insists upon the necessity of always distinguishing between justification and sanctification."

Under the influence of the Renaissance and Scholasticism, Melanchthonian tendencies did appear to some extent and they were carried to their extreme by the Scholastics of the Seventeenth century on the continent. One must remember that the Scholastics conceived of justification as a process by which a sinner was slowly transformed into a righteous man and because of justification emerged as an entirely new creature.

After their period of greatest activity had passed, the influence of Melanchthon in laying stress upon sanctification in dogmatic writing apparently diminished. The Puritanism of early America would be an indication of the movement but that is outside the pale of the Lutheran Church. Today one looks in vain among Lutheran works for deviations from Luther's idea of Justification by Faith as set forth in the historical confessions of the Church or by the pen of Luther in some of his personal works. It would appear that the Lutheran Church has been more successful in impressing the modern generation of its followers with the typically Lutheran view of Justification by Faith, than has been the case with other matters of doctrinal interpretation. It should be reiterated that the differences of Melanchthon and Luther on this point are less clear or pronounced than on other doctrines. What deviation there has been toward Melanchthon is the type which has been presented here—an emphasis on sanctification. Professor Sasse bespeaks the Lutheran genius when he exclaims: "As long as the Law stands 'on the same footing' with the gospel, repentance with absolution, sanctification with justification, obedience with faith, it is no longer the doctrine of Justification which 'alone shows the way to the unspeakable treasure and right knowledge of Christ, and alone opens the door to the entire Bible. "

CHAPTER FOUR

The Formula

of

Concord

THERE are a number of factors pertaining to the Formula of Concord which distinctly set it apart from the other Lutheran Confessions. For one thing, it is the last of the symbols of the Lutheran Church to be written and adopted. Since its formal acceptance in 1577, no confession or symbol has been adopted by the followers of Luther. In the second place, the Formula is an attempt to unify and consolidate the forces within Lutheranism, and was written for application to Lutheran bodies rather than primarily as a confession to the outside world of the doctrinal beliefs of the church. It was written to afford a common basis for Lutheranism in order to terminate an era of division and confusion within the Lutheran Church in Germany. To that end it was prepared with discriminating care and minute precision, as a body of teaching wholly Scriptural.

Again, the Formula of Concord is unique because it is the only one of the Lutheran Confessions written after the death of both Luther and Melanchthon, and therefore written without the personal and direct influence of either Reformer brought to bear upon it. Finally, it has failed to achieve world-wide adoption by Lutherans throughout the world, there being large sections of the church which never have required subscription to it, and do not today. We shall consider, later in this chapter, the acceptance or rejection of the Formula in various lands.

Luther's death came at a critical time in the history of the Reformation movement. There was much unrest among the various elements in Germany in the middle of the Sixteenth century. The peasants and common people were confused in their thoughts relative to the principles of the Reformation; and many strong leaders, who could not agree among themselves, were pulling in various directions, drawing others with them as well. Added to this was considerable political intrigue and the ever watchful eye of Rome, anxious to widen any breach which might appear among the Evangelicals.

Melanchthon was the logical successor to Luther as leader of the Reformation movement in Germany, but in spite of his amazing mental acumen and the merit of his writings he was no leader of men. It was a time which demanded a prophet who could fearlessly proclaim God's word and oppose with an iron will those who would confuse the Christian message or make its dissemination subservient to political ambitions. Thrust into the midst of a disrupted and confused movement, Melanchthon brought timidity and gentleness of character and an aversion to controversy into a situation which was certain to engulf and overwhelm such qualities. Lacking the heroic faith and stability of Luther, he was willing to conclude peace at any price. He who had proven his ability to see into the heart of theological controversies with such sharp insight, and who could deftly probe until he discovered error or deceit, was ready in these troubled times when those very qualities were needed most, to accept ambiguous phrases for clear confessions if only the opponents might thus be satisfied and peace be made to prevail. The result of his actions was still greater confusion at a time when the voice of authority and decision was the crying need of the hour. Krauth describes the results attending Melanchthon's ambiguity thus: "Much that he wrote could be taken in two senses. The Lutheran-Phillipists, who took the more charitable view, put the best construction on them, and were reluctant to abandon one to whom the Church owed so much, and whom Luther had loved so dearly. The Reformed put upon Melanchthon's words the construction most favorable to themselves. The Crypto-Calvinists made them their covert. The enemies of the Reformation appealed to them as proof that the first principles and doctrines of the Reformers had been abandoned. Whatever may be the meaning of Melanchthon's words in the disputed cases, this much is certain, that they practically operated as if the worse sense were the real one, and their mischievousness was not diminished but aggravated by their obscurity and double meaning. They did the work of avowed error, and yet could not be reached as candid error might. We have twenty-eight large volumes of Melanchthon's writings—and at this hour, impartial and learned men are not agreed as to what were his views on some of the profoundest questions of the Church doctrine, on which Melanchthon was writing all his life."

Both princes and theologians made several attempts to reunite a fast disintegrating church but they met with little success. Out of the various appeals and conferences there finally emerged a unifying factor which practically proved the salvation of the Lutheran Church in Germany. This factor was crystallized in final form in the Formula of Concord. If ever the Lutheran Church had faced a crisis it was during the period which ended with the adoption of Lutheranism's sixth particular creed. We now consider briefly the manner in which it came into existence.

In 1573 James Andreae of Tuebingen, who was issuing a second edition of his book on sects outside the Lutheran Church, added six chapters dealing with the controversies within Lutheranism. He sent copies to a number of theologians who approved of his writing, as did also the faculty of Tuebingen. The book had been dedicated to Duke Julius of

Brunswick who now sought to use this writing as a basis for amalgamating the various groups. He commissioned Martin Chemnitz to secure the approval of other theologians. When the approvals and the suggestions were received, certain revisions were adopted. After several conventions had been held and many eminent men consulted, there appeared a final draft which became known as the Swabian-Saxon Concord.

Shortly after this there appeared also the Maulbrunn Formula which had been composed by Lucas Osiander and Bidembach. Their work was done at the request of Louis, duke of Wuertemberg; Margrave Karl of Braden; and Count Ernest of Henneberg—three men who wished to present a statement to the Elector of Saxony for use in determining the orthodoxy of his theologians. When the Swabian-Saxon Concord and the Maulbrunn Formula reached the Elector of Saxony he decided, upon the advice of Andreae, to whom the Elector turned for counsel, to call a council of the distinguished theologians. It was his desire to submit to this body the two manuscripts he had received and let them formulate a final basis of agreement. The product of this convention is called the Torgau Book because the meeting had been held at Torgau.

Next, the Elector of Saxony sent copies of the Torgau Book to the other Lutheran princes and cities, with the request that they offer any criticism which they deemed necessary. When these critical suggestions were received and utilized in a revised edition of the book, it was called the Bergen Book, after the name of the place of meeting for the task of revision. The Elector now submitted this book as a formula of Concord to all the Lutheran princes and city councils as a final test of Lutheran orthodoxy and an authoritative interpretation of the Augsburg Confession. As many as agreed with it were to add their signature to the list of those approving. Though it was not accepted with unanimity, the Formula of Concord was adopted by a preponderant majority. The list of signatures bore the names of three Electors, twenty-one Princes, twenty-two counts, twenty-four Free Cities, and eight thousand teachers of the Church.

Thus ended a critical period through which the Lutheran Church had passed in safety. And it may well be said that not only for the Lutherans, but for the entire Protestant movement as well, a most precarious situation was now abolished. A threat of chaos, as a result of spreading heresy, was eliminated. Coming at a critical moment in the growth of the Reformation, the Formula of Concord practically saved Protestantism by meeting an entire series of crises in the realm of doctrinal beliefs. A threat from within, the most insidious of all forms of attack was overcome, and stability was guaranteed to the Lutheran Church, the mother of Protestantism.

When one considers the circumstances out of which the Formula of Concord was born, it is clear that the Formula would *a priori* turn from Melanchthon to Luther. When the Formula was produced the leaders realized it was no time either for compromising, middle-of-the-road views, or for meaningless phrases to be employed. The time had come to unite Lutherans by definitely eliminating the non-Lutheran influences which were proving to be such disruptive forces, as well as all compromising features which were only bewildering many of the people and leaving them subject to greater influences of other bodies. The era of Melanchthonian mildness had passed. Accordingly, the later and broader views of Melanchthon were not received favorably.

Already in the introduction to the Epitome of the Formula the conservative element is seen. For there is stated the rejection of the later editions of the Augsburg Confession by a subscription to the unaltered Confession. "Moreover as to the schism in matters of faith which has occurred in our time, we regard the unanimous consensus and declaration of our Christain faith and confession, especially against the Papacy and its false worship, idolatry, superstition, and against other sects, as the symbol of our time, viz., *The First Unaltered Augsburg Confession*, delivered to the Emperor Charles V. at Augsburg in the year 1530, in the great Diet, together with its Apology, and the *Articles* composed at *Smalcald* in the year 1537, and subscribed by the chief theologians at that time."

The second article of the Formula, dealing with the subject of free will, rejects the Philippistic view which taught that man's will was an aid used in conversion. In rejecting this view the Formula said that there are not three, but only two different causes of conversion, the Holy Spirit, and, as His instrument, the Word. Thus the Epitome asserts: "Concerning this subject, our doctrine, faith and confession is, that, in spiritual things, the understanding and reason of man are (altogether) blind, and, from their own powers, understanding nothing, as it is written (I Cor. 2:14): 'The natural man receiveth not the things of the Spirit of God; for they are foolishness to him; neither can he know them, because he is examined concerning spiritual things.'

"Likewise we believe, teach and confess that the will of unregenerate man is not only turned away from God, but also has become an enemy of God, so that it has inclination and desire for that which is evil and contrary to God, as it is written (Gen. 8:21): 'The imagination of man's heart is evil from his youth.' Also (Rom. 8:7): 'The carnal mind is enmity against God, for it is not subject to the Law of God, neither indeed can be.' Yea, as unable as a dead body is to quicken and restore itself to bodily, earthly life, just so unable is man, who by sin is spiritually dead, to raise himself to spiritual life, as it is written (Eph. 2:5): 'Even when we were dead in sins he hath quickened us together with Christ'; (II Cor. 3:5): 'Not that we are sufficient of ourselves to think anything, as of ourselves, but our sufficiency is of God.'"

Whether this is a rejection of Melanchthon or not is a conclusion which is not to be reached in haste if at all. There is no doubt that these statements in

the Formula are opposed to the teachings of the followers of Melanchthon, but the point has been raised
that his students erred in their interpretation of
their teacher's views on this subject. Hence George
Fritschel writes that "The pupils of Melanchthon
(already during his last years) misunderstood their
teacher and adhering to his phraseology, developed
into a heresy. In the Augsburg Confession (see especially in the Apology, Article XII) Melanchthon had
defined 'conversion' as 'repentance,' which, according to the Lutheran doctrine, is the product of the
Law and Gospel. Repentance or conversion is composed of two parts wrought by the Holy Spirit in the
human soul: contrition and faith. Later on, however, following his traditionalistic propensities, Melanchthon used the term 'conversion' in the wider
sense of Augustine to denote the whole change
wrought by the spirit throughout the entire life of a
man, both before and after justification.

Those who followed Melanchthon failed to realize
the significance of this change and consequently took
a wrong course which led them to synergism. Thus,
they claimed that as soon as the Spirit begins His
work in a human heart, and prior to justification,
man is able to cooperate in, and make a contribution
to, his own conversion. When Lutherans branded
this idea as Roman semi-pelagianism, the Philippists
bitterly defended their views.

Confusing the Philippists in all their teachings
with the views of Melanchthon would be a blunder-
ing error. On the subject of free will they carried

to extremes some of Melanchthon's statements and misunderstood him on others, as Fritschel pointed out. But the refutation of the Philippists in the second article of the Formula is more the rejection of that to which Melanchthonian tendencies on the subject lead, than of the views of Melanchthon himself.

Article four of the Formula of Concord, dealing with good works quotes several statements made by George Major, Justus Menius and others, based on expressions of Melanchthon. Again note, that the statements condemned are not those of Melanchthon, but of some of his more zealous followers. It is quite possible that if Melanchthon had been present in 1577 he too would have joined in the denunciation of those remarks. The statements specifically referred to in the Formula are the following: "Good works are necessary for salvation." "It is impossible to be saved without good works." "No one has ever been saved without good works."

In refuting these statements on the one hand, as well as the opposite extreme represented by Nicolaus Amsdorf who said "Good works are injurious to salvation" on the other, the Formula took the course of true Lutheranism explained in the chapter on Justification, namely, that good works have nothing to do with salvation but are nevertheless the inevitable fruit of faith. Thus the Formula states: "That good works certainly and without doubt follow true faith, if it be not a dead, but a living faith, as the fruit of a good tree.

"We believe, teach and confess also that good

works should be entirely excluded, as well when the question at issue is concerning salvation, as in the article of justification before God, as the apostle testifies with clear words, where it is written: 'Even as David also describeth the blessedness of the man unto whom God imputeth righteousness without works, saying . . . Blessed is the man to whom the Lord will not impute sin,' etc. (Rom. 4:6 ff.) And elsewhere, 'By grace are ye saved through faith, and that not of yourselves, it is the gift of God; not of works, lest any man should boast' (Eph. 2:8, 9).

"We believe, teach and confess also that all men, but those especially who are born again and renewed by the Holy Ghost, are bound to do good works . . . .

"Yet this should not be understood otherwise than as the Lord Christ and his apostles themselves declare, namely, that the liberated spirit does not do this from fear of punishment, as a slave, but from love of righteousness as children" (Rom. 8:15).

In regard to the phrase "good works are necessary to salvation," Melanchthon refused to sanction the phrase but would not condemn the author. The only thing such action might show is that he was mildly in opposition to such a view, whereas Luther would have thundered against it. The fact remains that he refused to sanction the statement.

Article seven deals with the Lord's Supper which was one of the principle subjects of controversy during the era in which the Formula was produced. On this point the Formula was very clear in what it did not believe. Though asserting themselves to be in opposition to the idea of oral manducation, the theologians emphasize that they believe it is the true body and blood received in the Supper. Thus, they "unanimously reject and condemn . . . that in the Holy Supper the body of Christ is not received orally with the bread; but that with the mouth only bread and wine are received, and the body of Christ only spiritually by faith."

On the other hand they do "believe, teach and confess that, in the Holy Supper the body and the blood of Christ are truly and essentially present, and are truly distributed and received with the bread and wine.

"We believe, teach and confess that the words of the testament of Christ are not to be understood otherwise than as they sound, according to the letters; so that the bread does not signify the absent body, and the wine the absent blood of Christ, but that, on account of the sacramental union, they (the bread and wine) are truly the body and blood of Christ . . . .

"We believe, teach and confess that the body and blood of Christ are received with the bread and wine, not only spiritually by faith, but also orally; yet not in a Capernaitic,* but in a supernatural, heavenly mode, because of the sacramental union; as the

---

*The word is derived from John 6:26, 52: "As though his flesh were rent with the teeth and digested like other food." Capernaitic is a term used several places in the Formula to express this meaning.

words of Christ clearly show, where Christ directs to take, eat and drink, as was then done by the apostles, for it is written (Mark 14:23): 'And they all drank of it.' Likewise St. Paul says (I Cor. 10:16): 'The bread which we break is it not the communion of the body of Christ?' i.e., he who eats this bread, eats the body of Christ, which also the chief ancient teachers of the Church, Chrysostom, Cyprian, Leo I., Gregory, Ambrose, Augustine, unanimously testify."

The Lutheran view of the Supper as set forth in the Formula and elsewhere presents the presence of Christ as a mystery, something not fully comprehensible to the human mind. It is a spiritual presence, in refutation of the Sacramentarians, yet the body and blood are received orally, in refutation of the Reformed. Lutherans deny transubstantiation as well as consubstantiation. Their doctrinal view in comparison to that of the Reformed and Roman Catholic is described thus; "From the standpoint of the Reformed doctrine the communicant receives nothing but bread and wine. From the standpoint of the Roman Catholic Doctrine, he receives nothing but the body and blood of Christ. For the Lutheran Church the bread remains bread and the wine remains wine, but the communicant receives with them, in an incomprehensible manner, the body and blood of Christ."

As we view the Formula of Concord in its entirety it appears that only in the articles mentioned is there any room for a conflict between Melanchthon and Luther. The broad view of the formula of Concord reveals that it mildly condemned Melanchthon. It opposed his mild manner by mincing no words in stating what the churches considered to be error and heresy. It was more the spirit of Melanchthon —that vacillating, compromising, peace-loving nature so characteristic of him—which the Formula rejected, rather than his theological views. However, it did very strongly condemn the extremes to which those men went who took the name of Melanchthon. These Philippists went to the radicalism which Luther had foreseen would result if some of Melanchthon's views were fully developed. The Formula cannot be said to reject Melanchthon when it accepts as a basic confession of the church the great symbol of the church which the learned theologian wrote. However it did return from the later Melanchthon to the earlier one—the man who was guided in thought and writing by the strong hand of Luther.

The Melanchthon of later life, whose spirit is rejected, was a man too tolerant of a laxity in doctrine and conviction. He would have been liberal where precision was demanded, and would accept human authority at the cost of minimizing the Word. Elements of humanism, rationalism and Romanism were all apparent in his conciliatory writings. It was this spirit which the Formula rejected, while retaining Melanchthon's well formulated doctrines of earlier days. It established his earlier works as the rock of confessionalism in the church but in so doing turned away from his later extremes. That is

the thought which impresses this writer in review-
ing the history and the material of the Formula of
Concord.

However, even if the Formula be considered a
rejection of the views of Melanchthon, still such
rejection did not receive universal approval. Many
lands did not formally accept the Formula, including
Denmark and Norway. The adoption of the Formula
by Sweden is not clear. Thus Dr. J. L. Neve writes:
"Sweden since 1649, included it (the Formula)
among the symbolic writings that were to be obliga-
tory for the ministry. This action was confirmed
in 1663 and 1686. But in a new constitution of
1809 the Augsburg Confession only is mentioned.
The uncertainty as to whether the whole Book of
Concord is binding for Sweden or not has given
rise to sharp controversies. A final decision has not
yet been made."

In America the majority of Lutherans have adopted the Formula but there are some exceptions
among those bodies which include the immigrants
and their descendants from the Scandinavian countries. Thus the Norwegian and Danish bodies subscribe only to the unaltered Augsburg Confession
and the Small Cathechism of Luther.

This fact must also be weighed in turn, before
passing judgment. Many lands did not adopt the
Formula of Concord because it was not urged upon
them for adoption. There was no attempt to
spread the Formula beyond Germany. It had been
composed in order to reunite a widely separated and

divided church in the land of Luther and having served the purpose for which it was intended, there was no need for its further extension. "The Princes and theologians by whom the Formula of Concord had been given to the world, had made no effort to procure the subscription and cooperation of the Churches outside of the German Empire. The reasons for this course were various. First, to have invited the co-working of other nationalities, would have complicated, to a degree of impracticability, what was already so tangled. Second, the difficulties which originated the necessity for the Formula of Concord were comparatively little felt outside of Germany. The whole doctrinal Reformation outside of Germany was in a certain sense secondary. Germany was the battle ground of a great struggle, and others waited, knowing that the decision there would be a decision for all. Third, Political barriers existed. In some lands where the Lutheran Church had strength, the rulers were Reformed or Roman Catholic."

In the light of what has been said, the Formula of Concord is seen to be a many-sided problem from the standpoint of the consideration of this paper. The statement that the Formula sides with Luther against Melanchthon, or the statement that it vindicates Melanchthon, must in either case be made with serious qualifications, and in the light of the considerations which have been made herein.

Choice of a Way

U NDER the title "More Dogma, Please" a call to his fellow clergymen of America to return to the clear teaching of the basic Christian doctrines was issued by an eminent member of the profession near the close of 1938. That call may well be prophetic, for there are signs that the next decade or two will see a strengthening of the doctrinal supports which give foundation and stability to Christian teaching and preaching. This movement will be of importance to the figures of Luther and Melanchthon because of the positions which they represent. The article stated above was no defense of fundamentalism, but a frank recognition that the modern era had gone too far in breaking with historic and accepted subjects of theological discourse. The writer noted that "The teaching of doctrine occupies a very small place in con-

temporary Christian preaching," and as one example
he pointed to the Harper's Monthly Sermon Library,
"to which fifty contemporary preachers have contributed each a volume of ten spiritual discourses.
One has only to read (these) . . . to see how few
sermons there are which deal with fundamental
Christian teaching." Dr. Bell quoted a layman friend
of his as saying after examining the fifty volumes in
the series mentioned: "They are almost all concerned,
these reverend gentlemen, in urging their hearers to
apply Christianity to this or that problem, individual
or social; but no stranger to Christianity, hearing
their sermons would gain a glimmer of an idea as to
what that Christianity is which they wish to see
applied. Do you suppose their congregations really
know?" One wonders if the ministers themselves
know.

A distinguished European scholar, after traveling
in this country, made the observation: "The American theological college pays little attention to theology. Instead, it gives a disproportionate deal of
time to two things: 'religious education' and 'Christian social service.' With some difficulty, I have
managed to find out what these are. 'Religious education' seems to be the art of imparting to others the
moral and devotional implications of a dogmatic
religion no longer existent. 'Social Service' seems to
be the advocated application to society at large of
ethical principles the validity of which is not of
necessity to be acknowledged in one's private life.
There is no fault to be found with religious educa-

tion, provided one has a religion in terms of which to educate. Nor is Christian social service a thing to be neglected, provided one has a Christian philosophy on the basis of which one desires to construct and manage society. As derivatives of theology, both have meaning; as substitutes for theology, they are empty wind."

"Be that as it may, a vast number of clergymen do not know what are the accepted principles of the Christian religion. If they are persuaded that they should preach doctrine, they do not even know where or how to begin."

The Church is now exhibiting signs which show it is awaking to the realization that in giving up its doctrinal emphasis it has cut itself off from an anchor which is necessary if the church is not to be blown about by every wind and fancy. Dogma enables one to state what he believes and why. The church is awaking also to the fact that while many of its clergy and therefore a large part of its people, due to the abandonment of doctrine in the past score of years, cannot give reasonable explanation of their faith, the enemies of the church—those "isms" which have sprung up in social, political, and religious environments—can most convincingly state their beliefs and the superiority of their views as well.

This writer is impressed with the shallow theological views of many clerics in the period since the war. This period has been one in which indoctrination is largely considered the thrusting of narrowminded views, verbatim, upon those under one's charge. It is

not uncommon to hear ordained men openly asserting their disavowal of Christ's divinity and the rejection of the ecumenical creeds of the church. If
such statements were made sincerely after the whole
problem and all that it involves had been carefully
analyzed, and with a full understanding of the periods and the problems which produced the great
creeds, one would credit them with an honest attempt to avoid hypocrisy. But one is moved to apply
the term hypocrisy instead to those who make such
statements, for the conclusions are not arrived at
after considerable thought and reading, as one might
presuppose when hearing time-accepted doctrines
decried—an act which involves considerably more
than many people appear to realize.

The desire for union of many denominations has
been very largely responsible for the act of discred-
iting theology and doctrine. In the desire to unite
Protestantism the point which has been too largely
overlooked is that every denomination has been
founded to preserve some Christian truth that was
threatened with extermination.

The world is in an era of crisis, both in politics
and in religion. Apparently the church is realizing
more and more that this is no time for superficial
optimism or shallow beliefs. It is a time when men
are asking heartfelt questions about both religion
and life. The masses seek authority while some denominations minimize authoritative sources of knowledge and guidance. Eminent men, both in the church

and out, are pointing to the fact that the church is no longer being sought for essentials of life. Thus Hendrick Kraemer speaks of this age as one of crisis for the church because it is being attacked at so many points. It is his contention that the *Corpus Christianum* has been shattering under the "progress of secularization in cultural, political and social spheres . . . religion and church seem so largely irrelevant to the bulk of man. It would take a whole chapter to describe the vicissitudes of the life of the Church in this whole situation, its shameful defeats, its silent victories, its lack of discernment, its ignoring of its real nature and mission, and its groping for light. . . . The confusion in which the Church finds itself, since its meeting and conflict with modern culture, modern thinking and modern organization of life, is from the viewpoint of the history of civilization the consequence of this gradual shattering of the *Corpus Christianum.* The Church has thereby lost its 'recognized' or 'established' position in the conscience of man, although the remnants of this 'established' position are still alive in the structure of modern society. This loss of the 'recognized' position in the conscience of man constitutes the present crisis of the Church as to its position in the world. The disintegrated masses, in their hunger for new authorities and symbols to give meaning to life, did not think for a moment of turning to the Church, but turned away from it. This is the first principle fact the Church has to face." Dr. Kraemer also notes the ray of hope, however, and asserts that "there are signs of the Church awakening to the real fundamental issues."

The Lutheran Church has always been a doctrinal church. Its emphasis upon this subject has diminished during the last score of years much less than the majority of Protestant bodies. Still it has not been completely sheltered from the swirling forces which have swept across religion, with the result that there has been a diminishing respect by its people, both lay and cleric, for the church's doctrine. That some have been influenced by non-Lutheran sources cannot be disputed. Shallow theological thinking of the present era has penetrated Lutheranism sufficiently to make deviations from official views quite an easy transition in certain instances. It has also opened the way for much greater influences of Melanchthon's later theories to be exerted upon the church. The official formulations of the Lutheran Church follow pretty much of a straight line from the Reformation to the present, remaining quite consistently with Luther. The exceptions are to be found almost entirely among individuals, rarely in confessions and theological utterances of the various bodies of Lutherans. It is the opinion of this writer that a returning interest in doctrine will bring with it a rediscovery of the vitality and accuracy of Luther's views when properly understood, and will end many of the Melanchthonian tendencies and much of the confusion in the church.

This volume has examined the contention of some

that Luther has been misunderstood. Doubtless he has, to a degree varying in each generation. It should also be emphasized that Melanchthon was misunderstood, greatly so, and that theological ideas and religious concepts were attributed to him which never should have been in all justice. It appears that certain radical followers of Melanchthon carried his name farther afield than any group of Lutherans have deviated from a course in harmony with Luther's views. In studying the deviations from Luther to Melanchthon one must be most careful in making sure he has determined Melanchthon's actual views on the point in question. Briefly let us recall the points at which the two Reformers stood opposed to one another, either openly or as evidenced in less emphatic ways.

Two men of opposite temperament and personality cooperated to bring into being within the Christian Church a movement which they sincerely understood to be a return, from a variety of adulterations, to pure Christian teaching. They firmly undergirded this movement which they inaugurated with evangelical fervor and Scriptural theology. Working together in close accord, what one man lacked the other supplied, but the talents and equipments of both were needed to launch the great Reformation successfully.

Martin Luther experienced religion in his innermost feelings of heart and soul; these experiences of his colleague were carefully pondered over and weighed in the mind of Philip Melanchthon until they found expression in his writings. Because he had *experienced* condemnation for sin, followed by the sense of forgiveness through faith in Christ, Luther was unwavering in his teachings concerning salvation. But the talented literary genius of Melanchthon was needed to put those experiences into clear theological utterances, and receiving these truths either second hand, *i.e.*, from Luther, or on the basis of a rational approach, Melanchthon was more prone to doubt the finality and validity of the doctrinal statements which the Reformation produced. Luther was sure of his ground and could say, "I know this is right, for I myself have experienced it." Melanchthon was inclined to wonder if all logical proof had been considered and the suggestions of all men properly and duly weighed before theological statements had been written. Luther felt there could be more clear and complete expressions of what he was giving to the world, but nothing more true, for he had discovered eternal truth.

The element of Humanism, and the element of Scholasticism as well, becomes a distinguishing feature in the two men. Melanchthon bore definite signs of such influence while Luther did not. Although originally allied with Erasmus, Luther's breach with him in 1525 when he published *De Servo Arbitrio* was inevitable owing to the fundamental differences in their point of view. The feud between Luther and Erasmus is a product of the German revolt against Latin hegemony, just as was the Kulturkampf of Bismark and the subsequent feud between the Roman and German lawyers. As for Scholasticism, the later

years of his life witnessed Melanchthon drawing ever
farther away from Luther's contempt for it. On this
point Dr. Otto Piper states the situation very clearly.
"The change in the different editions of Melanchthon's most important theological work, the *Loci
Communes,* is significant. The first edition limits itself to a description of God's work in man, and man's
experience of it by faith, and Melanchthon deliberately renounces the investigation of the mystery of
the Trinity and the Incarnation. He thinks that these
mysteries are accessible only by adoration. But in
every one of the following editions to an increasing
extent he tried to copy the speculations of the scholastics on these problems. . . .

"Moreover, the second generation of Lutheran theologians neglected entirely his (Luther's) methodical
aims in theology, though they emphasized the authority of 'Father Luther.' For a hundred years, down to
the second third of the seventeenth century, there is
in Germany the unshaken domination of a Protestant
scholastic theology.

"Several reasons co-operated in the development
of this theology. The Reformation of the Church is
contemporary with the movements of the Humanists, which tended to a new and deeper understanding of classical literature and philosophy. The Reformation owes to the Humanists some philological and
spiritual basic elements. On the other hand, leading
men of the Reformation, especially Melanchthon,
took an active place in this movement. Luther was
only willing to recognize the purely external value of

the movement—namely, the improvement of philological knowledge. Yet Melanchthon attributed propaedeutic and methodical value to classic philosophy, especially to Aristotle. Then, by and by, from slow progress in the first stages to an increasing speed in later times, Melanchthon substituted the Greek idea of science for the Lutheran idea of truth and divine knowledge."

Another distinguishing factor in the two Reformers is their differing approach to Unionism. Melanchthon was willing to speak softly of theological differences in order to unite the various branches of the church, while Luther disdained organic union and felt that only on the basis of doctrinal agreement should the different bodies be brought together. The latter's sentiment is reflected by Dr. Krauth in the statement "Truthful separation is far better than dishonest union, and two churches are happier, and more kindly in their mutual relation, when their differences are frankly confessed, than when they are clouding with ambiguities and double meanings the real divergencies." On this point the church has followed Luther completely. It is a matter which is settled by the church at large, not individuals, and the church at large seems to be bound with Luther's strictures where individuals are not. Accordingly the Lutheran Church in Germany struggled against a union with other groups which Hitler would bring about by force without any regard for theological or doctrinal differences. In Canada the Lutherans are not in the United Church. In the United States they were hesi-

tant about affiliating with the National Council of
Churches of Christ in America and with the World
Council of Churches, doing so only after certain
changes they had suggested were incorporated in the
constitutions of those bodies.

Another contrast is found in Melanchthon's vacillating quality as compared to Luther's stability. Indoctrination has given a stable character to the Lutheran Church, but only in regard to its theological
beliefs. Outwardly it is characterized by freedom and
moderation, insisting upon no one form of church
government. The Lutheran Church follows the type
of government of the land in which it is located. In
America it has the democratic form whereby presi-
dents of Synods and of the church at large are
elected to office at conventions of the church. In
Scandinavian countries, as in Germany and elsewhere in the world, the Bishopric is established.
Neither does the church demand acceptance of any
particular ritual, though much the same form is used
universally. Further, it does not limit the Gospel to
any ceremonial, such as baptism by immersion, or to
any one type of experience, either emotional, voli-
tional or intellectual. Many forms of organization,
wide diversities of practice and Christian experience
are found all over the world among Lutherans, the
largest denomination in the Protestant Church. It is
enough for the unity of the Church that the Gospel
be preached in its purity and the Sacraments rightly
administered. The denomination is not so fundamental that liberals break off from it, nor so loose

that fundamentalists are aroused. It harks back to established custom and belief sufficiently so that it is not engulfed by each new passing zeal and fancy, yet appears sanely progressive through the centuries.

While the two men were closely associated, the firmness of Luther held Melanchthon in bounds, but when out from under the influence of his elder, the younger man tended into certain unharmonizing positions, partly the result of rationalizing, partly because of his great love for peace which made him willing to compromise his views. This was true during the period from 1530 to 1540, again shortly following Luther's death. It was during those periods that Melanchthon's influence as opposed to Luther's is most evident, as well as in the Scholasticism on the Continent in the Seventeenth century. The only other pronounced period of Melanchthonian influence in the Lutheran Church was in the middle of the Nineteenth century in America in the movement which became known as American Lutheranism.

But influences may well exist even though they are not particularly obvious to the majority of those concerned. This volume has examined the charges that the church unknowingly followed Melanchthon on the doctrine of the Atonement, arriving at the conclusion that the main body of Lutherans did not do so, although some did. It is chiefly in stressing the importance of the law in Lutheran theology that these charges take root. The Lutheran Church has taken a course which cannot justly be called Nomism nor anti-Nomianism. It recognizes the service ren-

dered by the Law but that service is not to be
thought of as having any relation to the Atonement.
Aulén's volume serves as a warning to Lutherans to
be on the alert lest they stray from Luther on this
point.

The Augsburg Confession, though written by Melanchthon, was originally composed with the full approval of Luther and the Church. Later editions con-
tained changes which were challenged as being at
variance with the accepted edition. In most lands
the altered edition was either rejected from the start
or later discarded for the unaltered edition known
as the *Editio Princeps*. Hungary, Poland, and the
United States were the lands in which the greatest
tendency to follow Melanchthon on the Augsburg
Confession was revealed.

In the doctrine of Justification by Faith, Melanchthon tended to stress sanctification and good works,
while the fundamental Lutheran position holds that
the Gospel, justification, and faith are primary, and
only through them are the secondary elements of
Law and sanctification to be estimated or explained.
The idea of man's utter depravity is not popular at
the present time anywhere in the world. Lutherans
are under great temptation to desert this basic conception of Luther's, and at this point the greatest
possibility of swinging to Melanchthon, so far as this
doctrine is concerned, is to be found.

The Lutheran Church by nature is not one that
would be drawn into preaching the American socia'
gospel. Luther views the Church as the body of

Christ, and all organization and ecclesiastical hierarchy as a piece of the world. While the Church may take many forms in various denominations, these forms are not the Church itself which is spiritual. The task of the Church is in leading individuals to faith in Christ and thus opening to them the way of salvation. Through individuals society is to be regenerated. The church is to be separated from the state as its spiritual task is not something political but the right preaching of the Word and right administration of the sacraments.

Since the Lutheran Church frequently uses the term "Word rightly preached and sacraments rightly administered" does it consider itself the only denomination doing this? Dr. Evjen denied this and says, "Luther, as both Rudolph Sohm and Wilhelm Walther have shown, did not make this claim. Neither did the Augsburg Confession. Lutheranism knows only one church. Wherever the Gospel is preached *rightly,* this church is active. That is, the Life-of-Christ is active in the Holy Spirit. What does it mean to preach the Gospel rightly *(recte)?* It means to proclaim it in such a way that Christian life is awakened and nourished by it. Ministering the sacraments rightly means they nourish (not destroy) this life. Wherever this awakening and nourishing of the Christ-life takes place, the Church, or the Holy Spirit is operating."

The Formula of Concord partook of the uncompromising, battling spirit of Luther in place of the gentle, mediating view of Melanchthon. To some

extent the Formula of Concord rejected Melanchthonianism to return to Luther's concepts of the real
presence, in disclaiming freedom of man's will (even
to cooperate in conversion) and in specifically adopting the *Invariata* of the Augsburg Confession. In
these actions the church was simply following the
course which was generally to be pursued, namely,
that of bringing all theological formulations and confessions into line with Luther. The real deviations
were to be among individuals rather than the official
pronouncements of the church.

However, it is a gross error to think that one must
follow all the way with Luther in order to be a Lutheran. Luther himself denied this. He believed that
the Bible is our main authority and all others are to
be orientated to it. Further it was Christ in the Bible
who was the norm of authority. Thus some parts of
the Bible received little or no consideration from Luther since he judged them according to their revelation of Christ. He placed the Bible high above the
confessions of the church or his own writings. He
had found that the official doctrinal authorities of
the Catholic Church had not been able to give him
a satisfactory answer to his religious problems. This
led him to see that God's revelations were not re-
stricted to the hierarchy of the church. He believed
that in those who know God through the Bible, God
works His redeeming will. Therefore he plunged into
the work of giving the Bible to the common people.
He respected the letter of the Bible, realizing that
otherwise one may become victimized by his own

subjective opinions, but he did not worship the letter as some do today.

In April of 1522 Luther wrote an opinion on Communion *Sub utraque*. He published this together with essays concerning other innovations in the Church. Included in these published pamphlets are the following statements which give a very clear conception of what Luther considered to be the one norm and authority by which all other writings and individuals are to be judged. "As Paul says (Gal. 1:8) 'Though we or an angel from heaven preach any other gospel unto you than that which we have preached unto you, let him be accursed,' so say I, too, in the present case: In this and all other matters you must so firmly and surely build on the Word of God that you would not depart from it, even if—which God forbid!—I should turn fool and recant and deny my doctrine. In that event you must say: Though Luther himself or an angel from heaven should teach other doctrine, let it be accursed. For you must be the disciple, not of Luther, but of Christ. It is not sufficient to say: Luther, Peter, or Paul has said so, but you must feel Christ in your own heart, and you must be conscious without faltering that you have the Word of God, even though the whole world should fight against it. Until you feel this, you surely have not yet tasted the Word of God. Your ears still cling to the mouth of a man, or your eyes to his pen; you have not yet embraced the Word with your inmost heart, and have not grasped the meaning of Matthew 23:10: 'One is your master, even Christ.'

The Master teaches in the hearts of His disciples, however, through the external word of His preachers, who convey it to the ear; but it is Christ who drives the Word home. Hence, consider that you are facing persecution and death. In those trials I cannot be with you nor you with me. Everyone must fight for himself and overcome the devil, death, and the world. If in that emergency you were to look about to see where I am, or I where you are, and were to surrender your faith because you were told that I or some one else had taught a different doctrine, you would perish; for you would have allowed the Word to slip out of your heart; you would not be found clinging to the Word, but to me or others. There would be no help for you then."

The Lutheran Church believes the confessions to be of great value because they represent the best minds of an earlier day meeting problems which arose and had to be dealt with efficiently. To ignore their worth would be stubborn and foolish. However, they are secondary to the Bible, are to be judged in the light of the Bible (its knowledge of Christ), and discredited to whatsoever extent they are not in conformity to Biblical truth.

Lutherans have deviated from the views of Luther and will continue to do so, some being influenced by Reformed or Catholic principles, others following the lead of Melanchthon. Partly this has been due to a misunderstanding of Luther's views, partly because of an honest belief in the supremacy of other interpretations. The latter case does not seem to be as general as the former. Still others have departed from the Reformer to some extent and yet have remained good Lutherans in the proper sense of the word. But it is the opinion of many men who have studied the situation that there is at present a general trend in the Lutheran Church which is carrying it back more closely to the concepts of Luther. Thus Dr. Vergilius Ferm, collecting ten treatises from as many prominent men in the various branches of the Lutheran Church in America, treatises dealing with the subject: "What is Lutheranism" reaches the conclusion that, "On the whole the movement is, 'back to Luther' in the interpretation of Lutheranism."

Dr. Otto Piper, lecturing in 1933 at Manchester University on Recent Developments in German Protestantism contended that German Protestants have rediscovered Luther, finding new evidence which more clearly reveals his insights, and as a result coming under his influence to a greater extent than ever before. He believes that "the new understanding of Luther is one of the most important facts in the history of modern German Protestantism. The New Theology has attained quite a new and, we may add, an adequate understanding of Luther. In as far as prewar theologians had a religious or a theological interest in Luther, they usually ascribed to him their own ideas, or at least neglected anything in Luther which was not in harmony with their own conception of Protestantism.

"The new understanding of Luther was favored by two facts: (1) the discovery of new and important

documents which threw new light on Luther's religious development; and (2) the new method of
historical interpretation." He explains the first of
these by saying, "The most important event in modern research on Luther was doubtless the discovery
of his lectures on the Epistle to the Romans of 1515-
1516. For these lectures not only mark the decisive
change in his religious and theological attitudes, but
also reveal better than any later document the main
forces of his religious life."

The new era which the church is now entering
gives promise of being one in which there will be a
return to dogma throughout the entire world. Wherever the existence of the church is being challenged
it is being driven to build sound doctrinal foundations in order to have something to stand upon as an
excuse for its existence. And the Church is everywhere being asked more and more why its continued
existence is justified. In this era it is natural that Luther will be re-examined, especially by those bear-
ing his name. His views will be carefully thought
through once again, and though he will not be accepted *in toto*, still his influence will once more in-
crease. Along with him, Melanchthon will likewise
loom larger, as the author of the greatest theological
documents which the Reformation produced. It will
not be the later Melanchthon, however, who will
emerge, but the man who wrote the *Loci* of 1521 and
the Augsburg Confession of 1530. Even now the
pendulum is swinging from the traits characteristic
of Philip in his later years to the Philippo-Lutheran

views of 1517-1530—the period which gave strong structural support to the Reformation during the time when, challenged to give reason for its existence, it answered with all the authority, weight, and influence of evangelical fervor and eternal, Scriptural truth.